# VIDEO GAMES ARE THE HOTTEST THINGS AROUND.

And the video game picture is constantly changing. But the games themselves are no fad. They are exciting, almost hypnotic entertainment. Millions of people are spending billions of dollars playing them every year. The technology of the games is always being improved. The games of tomorrow are going to be more colorful, more exciting and better all round than the games of today. Part of the excitement of the games is waiting to see what's next. In short, video games are here to stay.

So since you're going to spend the next few years of your life jiggling joysticks and pushing action buttons, you should know something about how the games work. And you're going to have to learn a few new words . . .

**And Daniel Cohen Tells You
All About Them!**

**Books by Daniel Cohen**

BIGFOOT: America's Number One Monster
CREATURES FROM UFO'S
FAMOUS CURSES
THE GREATEST MONSTERS IN THE WORLD
MISSING! Stories of Strange Disappearances
THE MONSTERS OF STAR TREK
REAL GHOSTS
SUPERMONSTERS
THE WORLD'S MOST FAMOUS GHOSTS
VIDEO GAMES

Available from ARCHWAY paperbacks

# Daniel Cohen

**AN ARCHWAY PAPERBACK**
Published by POCKET BOOKS • NEW YORK

AN ARCHWAY PAPERBACK *Original*

 An Archway Paperback published by
POCKET BOOKS, a Simon & Schuster division of
GULF & WESTERN CORPORATION
1230 Avenue of the Americas, New York, N.Y. 10020

ISBN: 0-671-45872-8

First Archway Paperback printing September, 1982

10 9 8 7 6 5 4 3 2 1

AN ARCHWAY PAPERBACK and colophon are
trademarks of Simon & Schuster.

Printed in the U.S.A.

IL 4+

# ACKNOWLEDGMENTS

A book like this can never be written without help and I would like to thank the following people for their co-operation: Donna M. Datre of Toy Manufacturers of America; Ed Williams and Gerald A. Michaelson of Magnavox/Odyssey; Beth Ramey and Barbara Wruck of Coleco Industries; Bill Kunkel of *Electronic Games*; Dianne Drosnes of Activision; Jeff Hoff of Atari; Joan Gasperini of Mattel Electronics; our photographer Rich Tarbell; and the real authorities, our panel of video game judges who destroyed all adult competition at a single twitch of the controls: Mark Williams, Samantha Quick, Theo Cohen, Joan Kearns, Wesley Wang, Shawn Parker, Kelly Shannon, George Towne, Sameer Desai, and David Decker.

# CONTENTS

# CHAPTER 1

# THE HOTTEST GAME IN TOWN

If you have been living in a very deep cave for the last four or five years you may never have heard of Pac-Man, or Space Invaders, or Asteroids or Donkey Kong or Tron.

If you come blinking and squinting out of your dark cave you may be temporarily blinded by the flashing lights and shifting colors. You will be confused by the beeps and bleeps and the little electronic jingles. You may be alarmed by the ominous electronic voices warning of an "alien intruder." And you will certainly wonder what all those people are doing pushing buttons, wiggling levers and throwing one quarter after another down a slot.

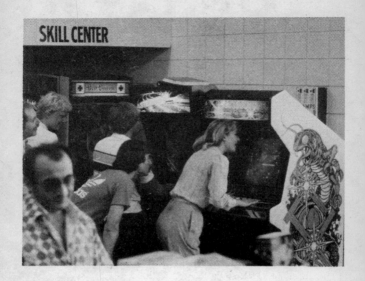

In short—if you have been completely out of touch you may never have heard of video games.

The rest of you know that video games are the hottest things around. You've already tossed down more quarters than you want to think about in the arcades. If you don't own a home video game, you want one; and if you do own one, you're anxiously waiting for the latest cartridges and looking forward to a new improved model of the game itself.

Most of the video game excitement has been created among the kids. But plenty of adults play the games, too. They just may not play as well. Have you seen that guy with the gray beard at the corner machine? He chunks down one quarter after another, but his games never seem to last more than sixty seconds. Don't laugh, that may be me.

While some adults love the games, others hate them and have tried to ban them. The games stir elemental passions one way or the other. The adults who love the games most of all are those who make them. Video games mean big, big bucks. If someone offers you stock in Atari or gold—take the Atari. It's better than gold.

Video games have not been around very long. The video game picture is constantly changing, but the games themselves are no fad. They are exciting, almost hypnotic entertainment. Millions of people are spending billions of dollars playing them every year. The technology of the games is always being improved, and the games of tomorrow are going to be more colorful, more exciting and better all around than the games of today. Part of the excitement of the games is waiting to see what's next. In short, video games are here to stay.

So since you're going to spend the next few years of your life jiggling joysticks and pushing action buttons, you should know something about how the games work. And you're going to have to learn a few new words.

The real experts toss around words like *software* and *microprocessors*. If you don't want to feel left out you had better know what they mean. Spend a few minutes with this book and you, too, can sound like an expert and really impress your friends.

The first word you have to learn is *computer*. A video game is basically a computer. I know a computer is supposed to be something that makes out the gas bill, but computers do lots of other things. One of the things they are best at is playing games.

Computers have a memory. In fact, they have two kinds of memory. The first is called the *Read Only Memory* or *ROM*. The ROM contains all the basic information about a game—what it's going to look like and what's supposed to happen.

The second type of memory is the *Random Access Memory* or *RAM*. RAM memory is short. It contains the score, the number of Pac-Men or buckets or spaceships you have left on your turn and so on.

All of the instructions for how a game is going to work are called the *program*. Programs are also called *software*. The arcade or coin-op games are specially designed to use a single program. You can play only one type of game on each machine.

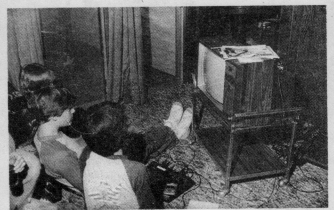

On your home video system you can play different games. It is "programmable." Each time you want to play a new game you put in a new cartridge. Now don't tell me that the cartridge you put in home video is hard, and then ask why it's called software. Programs are called software no matter what sort of container they come in.

The *hardware* is the computer itself. On a home video system, that's the console you plug the cartridge into. The guts and heart of the computer are tiny chips of silicon called *microprocessors*.

In many ways the tiny microprocessors are the real heroes of the video game story. Without them all of those greedy little gobblers and alien spaceships and barrel-throwing gorillas would never have been possible, or at least not very practical. Even though it was possible to build a video game twenty years ago, the game would have been the size of your room and would have cost thousands of dollars, since big computers were used for game playing at that time. With the microprocessors the machines could be brought down to reasonable size. They make the machines cheaper and more reliable. The silicon chips are also what make digital watches and electronic calculators possible.

Now you know about the hardware and software, but where do you—the game player—

come in? You are the *input*. When you move your joystick or press the action button or run your fingers over the keyboard, you send a message into the computer.

Let's say you move the joystick left. The message is "Pac-Man move left." The computer is also getting messages from the program. These messages say "Monsters catch Pac-Man—get to him by the shortest possible route." So the monsters move left. The machine reacts to you. You move up to get out of their way. You have to think and move faster than the machine. Every time Pac-Man eats a dot, that sends a message to the RAM. That message adds points to your score. There can

Rich Tarbell

be a lot of different messages going into the machine at the same time. But the computer can handle it.

All of this information—action and reaction, scores and number of gobblers left—is displayed on a video or television screen. That's where the name *video game* comes from. It takes only microseconds for this information to be displayed on the screen. Computers are very fast. The form the display takes—Pac-Man and the monsters, spaceships or a stupid gorilla, for example—depends on the program. The pictures are called *graphics*. The bangs, buzzes, little tunes and voices are all part of the program, too.

You are not going to react the same way every time. Neither will the computer. If the computer reacted exactly the same way every time you did something you would soon catch on. You could beat the machine easily. It wouldn't be much fun. Most programs have what is called a *Random Event Generator (REG)*. This means that sometimes you can predict what the computer will do, and sometimes you can't. It keeps you guessing. That's what makes a video game a real contest.

Okay, that's enough heavy information for a start. Now let's turn back the clock to those not so thrilling days of yesteryear. The years BP—Before Pong.

# Chapter 2

# The Sons and Daughters of King Pong

Legend around the arcades has it that the Age of Video Games began in 1972. It was then that a bright young computer technician named Nolan Bushnell introduced a game called Pong.

True enough, Bushnell's introduction of Pong was a great moment in video game history. But *Electronic Games,* the magazine of video and computer games, puts the beginning of the Age of Video Games ten years earlier.

"In 1962 Steve Russell, a graduate student at M.I.T. (Massachusetts Institute of Technology) decided that it would be great fun to create an entertainment program he could run on one of the school's . . . computers."

What Russell came up with was a game called Spacewar. It quickly became a great favorite with programmers all over the country. It provided a nice change from working with business and scientific problems.

Among those who spent a lot of time playing Spacewar were a couple of other M.I.T. students, Bill Pitts and Nolan Bushnell. Both of them thought that computer games might have commercial possibilities.

They both worked out versions of Spacewar. Bushnell's version was called Computer Space, Pitt's The Galaxy Game. Both games were tried out on the public. Neither was much of a success.

In the 1970s coin-operated computers were already in the arcades. But they were used for such things as a Computer Quiz. You put in your coin and picked a topic. A series of multiple-choice questions on that topic flashed on the screen. You chose your answer. The computer told you if you were right or wrong and totaled up the score. Computer Quiz was a simple and limited machine. It never attracted a wide following. It was too much like a quiz at school.

Bushnell wasn't ready to give up quite yet. He decided that the problem with his Computer Space game was that it was too complicated. Sure, it was the sort of thing that computer engineers liked to play, but most people out there were not computer engineers. The public wanted something quicker to learn—and more entertaining.

In 1972 Bushnell built a new game in his garage. It was called Pong. The name is one half of Ping-Pong—because that's what the game most resembled. A little electronic dot could be batted back and forth across the screen with electronic paddles controlled by the player. It was certainly simple.

Bushnell first tried to interest the Bally Corporation, the big pinball manufacturer, in Pong. The pinball men couldn't see it. They didn't think the game had a future. That was not one of history's great predictions. To be fair, very few thought video games had a future. And Bally was to recoup its error brilliantly in just a few years.

Bushnell had to go it alone. He formed his own company. He gave the company the name Atari. It's a Japanese word used in a game called Go. It means what checkmate means in chess.

Bushnell built a coin-op version of Pong. He tried it out in a Sunnyvale, California bar called Andy Capp's. The game was an immediate hit. It soon began turning up not only in arcades but also in pizza parlors, candy stores, bowling alleys and anyplace else kids might hang out.

Nolan Bushnell wasn't the only one working

on video games. The Magnavox Corporation of Knoxville, Tennessee was one of the big U.S. manufacturers of TVs. An engineer named Ralph Baer developed a home video game system. He had been working on such a system since 1966. He had showed the system to several manufacturers, and in 1972 he showed it to Magnavox. Magnavox bought it. The result was the Odyssey system; Odyssey was programmable. With it you could play about twenty games, including a Pong-like game. Some people believe that Baer, not Bushnell, should get the credit for developing Pong-style games.

Magnavox continued to improve Odyssey over the next few years. It sold, but it didn't take off. The world just wasn't ready for the home video game yet. But Magnavox didn't give up. They improved their system, and they managed to build up a modest home video business. Perseverance has paid off. Today Magnavox is one of the leaders in home video games.

As the technology improved, other companies got into the home video business. One of the most successful was Coleco. Coleco's Telstar Arcade was the favorite gift under a lot of Christmas trees in 1976.

Bushnell's Atari company made a deal with Sears. A home version of Pong was marketed

Early examples
of the
Magnavox/Odyssey
system

by the giant company. In many ways the Sears Pong wasn't as good as the other home video systems then available. But it was a lot cheaper. And it was generally simpler to operate and more reliable. The first arcade, or home game, most Americans played was Pong.

But Sears' Pong and Coleco's Telstar and all the other home games were just games. Kids played them and forgot them. The real glamour of video games today comes not from the home games of the mid-1970s but from the arcades.

Atari was still plugging away at the arcades. Bushnell developed a number of different types of driving, sports and battle games. His biggest hit after Pong was Breakout. *Electronic Games* says that it was a "significant advance over the early, crude, ball-and-paddle programs."

About this time Bally, which had originally turned down Pong, was beginning to wonder if it had made a mistake. Video games were turning up everywhere. People were dumping quarters into them instead of into the more traditional games like pinball. Perhaps video games were more than a passing fad. Bally put out a couple of video games of its own. One was called Gunfighter. Two cowboys shot electronic bullets at one another. Despite the Old West setting, the game had been developed in Japan.

Over in Japan some big-time game manufacturers were also becoming aware of video games. The Japanese are great game players. Their favorite game was Pachinko—a pinball-like game that you could bet on. There were Pachinko parlors all over the place. Restaurants and coffee shops all had Pachinko machines. Then, in 1978, Pachinko was suddenly in trouble.

The trouble was caused by a little electronics company called Taito Limited. Taito began marketing a game in which the player had to shoot down lines of funny-looking aliens. It wasn't just a target game. The aliens could shoot back. The name of the game, as you have doubtless already guessed, was Space Invaders. Space Invaders was the real breakthrough in popularity for video games in Japan, and in the United States as well.

The Japanese are among the world's leaders in electronic and computer technology. They also love science fiction. The combination of games, technology and science fiction was irresistible. Taito placed 100,000 games in the first year. The Japanese went crazy over the funny-looking little aliens. They spent some $670 million on the game. Almost overnight Space Invaders had pushed out the traditional Pachinko machines.

Instead of a quarter the Japanese machines use 100-yen pieces. The bank of Japan had to triple the production of 100-yen coins just because of Space Invaders.

What succeeds in Japan does not always succeed in the United States. But Bally's manufacturers decided that it might now be time for the big video game breakthrough. How right they were this time. Bally got the U.S. rights to Space Invaders in 1978. Over the next two years Bally manufactured more than 60,000 games. Space Invaders is no longer being manufactured. It hasn't been for a long time. But in most large arcades there are still one or two units around. A lot of arcaders still find it a challenging and exciting game. And there are those who play it for old time's sake.

Space Invaders created an industry all its own. There was, of course, a home video version of the game. There were small hand-held versions and slightly larger table-top versions. A Space Invaders program for home computers was sold. Tiny versions of Space Invaders were included in watches and calculators. There were Space Invaders posters and tee-shirts. And, of course, there were the inevitable Space Invaders imitators. In 1979 and early 1980, a visit to a video game arcade was like a visit to a family of Space Invaders clones. It seemed that practically every game was the science fiction, Space Invaders type. Space Invaders had made the public at large aware of video games. And a lot of people thought that was all there was to it. But the field didn't stand still.

For some three years Space Invaders reigned supreme in the arcades. Other games came and went, but most people still loved knocking off those little aliens. Then, in 1981, a new arcade game was introduced that knocked the popular Space Invaders out of its top spot. The game was Asteroids. The manufacturer was Atari.

Asteroids, too, was a science fiction type of game. The player scored by zapping things. The player was to imagine himself the pilot of a spaceship making its way through an asteroid swarm. He had to avoid the asteroids and destroy them before they hit him. He also had to avoid and, if possible, destroy hostile UFOs that were shooting at him, too.

The game sounds a lot like Space Invaders. But it didn't look like the old classic. And it didn't feel like Space Invaders, either. The dangers came at the player from all parts of the screen and at many different speeds. The player had more maneuverability. All of this was made possible by a new technical innovation called Quadrascan.

In theory Asteroids could be played forever on a single quarter. The newspapers were filled with stories of kids who had stayed on in front of the game for twelve or fourteen hours at a stretch and accumulated scores of up to thirty million points.

Asteroids also appeared as a hand-held

game, a home video game and a program for the home computer. There was a rush of Asteroids imitations into the arcades. Atari even imitated itself with Asteroids Delux. It was supposed to be an improved version of the original, but a lot of people preferred the original Asteroids.

By now you have probably noticed something. Practically all of the games we have talked about, except Pong, have been science fiction type games. Way back in 1972, the first popular game program was Spacewar. Then came Space Invaders and Asteroids and all their imitators. Science fiction games, and games in which the player scored by destroying things, completely dominated the arcade scene. Other types of games were possible. Other types were being produced. There were video sports games and driving games. But they were never as popular as the space war games. Why?

Tradition was part of the reason for the science fiction dominance. That's what people were used to. That's what they had come to expect. And for a while that was the type of game that the designers were best at making.

Then, too, computers and science fiction seemed to go together. Computers were futuristic technology. Science fiction was about the future. It was a natural combination.

The popularity of science fiction, particularly movies like *Star Wars*, also contributed a lot to the popularity of the games. The player could imagine himself to be Luke Skywalker maneuvering through space and zapping Darth Vader's ships.

Therefore it came as a big surprise that the next arcade-game superstar—the biggest video game to date—is as far removed from the science fiction type of game as Bugs Bunny is from Luke Skywalker.

That game is Pac-Man, and Pac-Man deserves a chapter all its own.

# CHAPTER 3

# PAC-MAN CONQUERS AMERICA

He was born in Japan, and there was no big fanfare when he came to America in 1981. Namco Limited, the Japanese company that invented him, figured he was too cute for a serious name, so they called him "Paku-Paku." Paku means to open the mouth and gobble in Japanese. By the time he'd crossed the ocean it was changed to Pac-Man. Say paku-paku fast a couple of times and you will see why the name was changed. The Bally company, which brought Space Invaders from Japan, also brought Pac-Man.

A lot of experts predicted he'd die fast once he got to the arcades. After all, what did he have going for him? He wasn't a war game or a sports game, an invasion-from-outer-space kind of game or a racing car game. No, he was a maze game. And there weren't many mazes among the top twenty video games before he came along.

Did he show them! The experts forgot that mazes have fascinated people since the time of the ancient Greeks, when the hero Theseus had to find his way to the center of a labyrinth (another word for maze) and kill the Minotaur, a scary, bull-like monster that lived there. Even today puzzle-makers put out lots of books of mazes. You solve these by drawing a pencil line through the maze until you escape from the other end. Any kid who's been in a house of mirrors or the haunted house at an amusement park has been in a form of maze. England's famous castle, Hampton Court, built by Henry the Eighth, has a maze built from bushes and shrubs. I once wandered around in it lost for an hour before I found my way out. So there is nothing new about the maze craze.

But the idea of a video character with charm was new. Bally's Pac-Man became the number-one success story, the superstar of video arcade games. According to the *Wall Street Journal,* nearly one billion dollars in quarters was devoured by Pac-Man coin-op machines in the game's first year in America. The home version of Pac-Man, manufactured by Atari, may make more money than the movie *Star Wars*. Pac-Man is expected to sell nine million cartridges in 1982 alone. The microchip itself costs about $1.50 to produce. Then there's another $1.50 to package the chip and pay Namco Ltd. in Japan for the rights to make the cartridge. Finally, there's money to be spent advertising Pac-Man. Still, with cartridges costing between twenty and forty dollars, we are talking about millions of dollars in profits. No wonder a lot of people think Pac-Man looks like a little round gold coin. He is fondly referred to by arcade owners as a "real quarter sucker."

The big question is why? What makes Pac-Man special? For one thing the controls are simple. Some of the arcade games are hard to play, requiring a lot of complicated maneuvers. Not so with Pac-Man, or Packy, as he is sometimes lovingly called. A simple four-direction joystick is all you have to worry about. Then there are the sound effects. He sounds different gobbling dots from when he's eating monsters. Speaking of monsters, Packy isn't the only one in the game with personality. They're pretty cute in their own right. Each is a different color, and their personalities are different, too. There's the terrifying Blinky, yellow-orange Clyde, the fast-moving Pinky and Bashful (alias Winky).

Then there are the prizes: bells, medals, keys, gold and silver bars, depending on your level of skill. And the halftime shows are little cartoon skits that make the game even more fun. Pac-Man presents supergraphics, not the kind that dazzle you in a cold, science fiction way, but very human, very personal. The same thing that makes us love the cartoon characters on Saturday morning television makes us love Pac-Man and the monsters. They make us think they're real.

One of the big reasons for Pac-Man's popularity is that girls like him just as much as boys. Before Pac-Man, arcades were mostly for boys who liked to play the space zap games. A lot of people thought that would never change. Even arcade owners were surprised when girls started showing up to play Pac-Man. Of course, girls' interest in video games wasn't caused just by Pac-Man. Video games had spread to restaurants, airports, supermarkets, convenience stores—places that weren't strictly boys' territory—and the girls started to play them.

This was the best thing that could have happened to video games because manufacturers of the games came to realize that there was a huge, untapped audience for their product. They had to redesign their games to reach that audience, and that meant coming up with new concepts, developing a wider range of ideas. One result of this is Ms. Pac-Man.

She has long eyelashes and wears a bow in her hair. But she's just as hungry as Packy himself. In a way she's more of a challenge than old Packy because her maze changes every other board. Still, never underestimate Pac-Man. According to Bally officials, new variations are in the works. One involves a maze that disappears when Pac-Man eats an energizer. Try that one if you think the present maze is tough.

The big news in the world of Pac-Mania in the spring of 1982 was the introduction of home video Pac-Man games. Since everybody seems to like Pac-Man—girls, boys, old people, kids in kindergarten—Pac-Man cartridges sold like crazy.

Stores were taking orders way in advance. When the cartridges finally arrived, crowds formed and Pac-Man was sold out on the spot. Any kid who was first on his block to own an Atari home video Pac-Man cartridge felt like the luckiest kid in town.

Of course, home video Pac-Man is not the same as arcade Pac-Man. Instead of monsters you have ghosts, though they look just about the same. Pac-Man himself is no longer all mouth. He has an eye. Some people complain that the home video model lacks the personal-

Promotion for Atari home video Pac-Man

ity of the arcade game and that the controls are difficult. Still, I found myself hooked on home video Pac-Man the day I was at last able to find a cartridge at our local department store.

The controls take a little practice, but after you get the hang of them you'll find you move from level three to level six quickly. And it's exciting. The running ghosts really lead you a merry chase.

Of course, you reverse all that when you become the hunter and chase them. Maybe that's part of Packy's appeal, too—the ability to switch places in the same game, to be both pursuer and pursued and still remain the same character.

Will there ever be a better game than Pac-Man? Perhaps its unusual blend of being easy to learn yet requiring skill and strategy to play will never be repeated, or at least not repeated in such an irresistible cartoon character as Pac-Man. As you guide Pac-Man across your television screen you see the entire game constantly from his point of view. In a way you are Pac-Man. Psychologists have a word for this: identification. It's going to be tough for video game manufacturers to come up with a better character to identify with than Pac-Man.

They know it, too, which is why Pac-Man has moved from the arcades to home video and even into battery-operated electronic games. Coleco has introduced a table-top variation of Pac-Man for kids eight years old and up. There is a nonelectronic board game version of Pac-Man. Video game manufacturers have accused each other of stealing the Pac-Man idea and making imitations of the original. There's a lawsuit going on right now with Atari and Bally on one side and Magnavox/Odyssey on the other over the company's cute little chewer, K. C. Munchkin. But lawsuits are inevitable in

## K.C. MUNCHKIN!

How many Munchies can your Munchkin munch
before your Munchkin's all munched out?????
Myriads of different mazes!

any new field where the rules are still being
worked out, and home video only goes back a
very few years. Though it has hit the world
with the force of a giant, the video game industry is still in its infancy. There have already
been plenty of lawsuits, and there will be more.

Now, one last question. Is Pac-Man just a fad? Will you forget all about him until one day a few years from now you reach into your closet and find an old Pac-Man tee-shirt and say, "Hey, I remember him"? It's too early to tell, of course, even though Pac-Man has inspired hit songs like "Pac-Man Fever," Columbia Records' hit, decorated towels, appeared in books and is slated to appear on pajamas, towels, trays, you name it. Furry Pac-Man dolls are in the offing.

Will it all blow over or will Pac-Man join the ranks of the immortal superstars of our time, like Snoopy and Miss Piggy? Well, like I said, it's too early to tell, but you wouldn't catch me betting against the little fellow with the big mouth.

Save those Pac-Man shirts.

# CHAPTER 4

# WHERE HAVE ALL THE PINBALLS GONE?

Once upon a time there were penny arcades. These were areas with a large selection of coin-operated machines. Penny arcades could be found mainly in amusement parks and vacation areas.

At first games were pretty simple. There were pellet guns for target shooting, mechanical claws that grabbed worthless prizes, and mechanical baseballs. Along with the games were coin-operated movie machines, fortune-telling machines and something called a "love tester." You squeezed a handle, and the machine was supposed to tell you what kind of a lover you were. It would light up with words like "Hot Stuff." That was hot stuff, fifty years ago.

The machine that came to dominate the arcade was the pinball machine. Pinball machines first made their appearance during the Great Depression of the 1930s. People needed cheap entertainment, a way to escape their troubles. But by that time the arcade wasn't a "penny" arcade anymore. Prices went up to a nickel, then a dime and finally a quarter. But whatever the price, the pinball remained king of the arcade.

In pinball the player uses a plunger to send a steel ball rolling around the playing surface of the machine. The ball hits various objects, called bumpers, or falls into holes, or rolls through "gates." Each of these events is worth a certain number of points, and each sends the ball shooting off in a different direction. A player can run up a huge score. Scores are displayed in lights on a glass panel in back of the machine.

Usually each coin buys the player five balls. If the score is really large, the player earns extra balls. The pinball wizard can play for quite a long time on a single coin.

In pinball the player can control the movement of the ball to a degree. Flippers, activated by buttons, knock the ball back onto the playing surface. The ball can also be moved around by gently lifting or pushing the machine. But not too hard. Too much movement and the word "Tilt" will light up on the back glass. Once the machine registers "Tilt," the game is over.

Pinball machines themselves are very colorful to look at. And during play lights flash and bells ring. Pinball was an exciting game, and it still is.

From the 1930s onward the pinball machine was the king of the arcades. Pinball also moved out of the arcades and machines were found in bus stations, bars and shopping centers. In the 1970s the machines even inspired music, a rock opera *Tommy* by the British group The Who. The hit song from *Tommy* was "Pinball Wizard." The song climbed to the top of the charts. And it inspired a burst of enthusiasm for pinball.

Pinball was popular, but it was never completely respectable. Adults complained that kids were wasting their time and money. They said arcades were sleazy places. Some towns banned pinball machines completely. Still people went on playing the games where and when they could. In the 1970s pinball was as vigorous as ever.

At first video games didn't seem to be much of a threat to pinball supremacy. (That's what the Pachinko manufacturers in Japan thought, too.) But by the 1980s king pinball had been dethroned throughout the arcades of America.

People are still playing pinball. And new machines are being made, over 100,000 in 1981. The new pinball machines are bigger, flashier and more gimmicky than ever. Some talk to you. Others are huge. They use baseball-sized steelies. But they can't compete for your quarter.

In most arcades there are a few pinball machines stuck in odd corners, just for old time's sake. The newer arcades sometimes don't have any pinball machines at all. Some children growing up right now may never see a real "live" pinball machine. Old machines are valuable. They sell as antiques.

The outside of a pinball machine is usually much flashier than the outside of the average arcade video game. The pinball machine makes a satisfying variety of buzzes and bongs. And they really are fun to play—for a while. But when you get right down to it, it doesn't matter if the game is called Ballyhoo (the name of the original pinball machine) or Dolly Parton (the name of one of the newer entries)—the game is basically the same. A little steel ball is rolling around the playing surface, and the player doesn't really have much control over what happens. The action in the video game varies enormously. And the player has far more control over the action and the score.

As we saw in Chapter 2, video games really

Atari® Asteroids Deluxe™ video game

began in the arcades. While home video games are becoming more popular and more sophisticated every day, the arcade remains the front line for the games. Many of the best home games are imitations or adaptations of popular arcade games.

Sometimes gamers are disappointed with the home version of their favorite arcade game. The controls are not as responsive. The graphics are not as brilliant. The sounds are not as clever. The game itself is not as complex. Some arcade snobs look down their noses at home games.

The two should not be compared. No home game can match an arcade game, for some pretty obvious reasons. The arcade game is a one-purpose machine. It is designed especially to play a single game. The average arcade game costs anywhere from $2,500 to $3,000. That's a lot more than your home game costs. And the arcade game is much bigger. It contains technology that simply can't be squeezed into a small console and a TV set. So no matter how good home video games get, they are not going to replace the arcade games for quite a while.

What makes a successful arcade game like Asteroids or Pac-Man? Nobody knows. Designers beat their brains out coming up with new gimmicks and new angles. Some of them catch on, some of them don't. The stakes are high. A big winner can create millionaires.

Here are some of the dollar figures behind the games. The average arcade game takes up about nine square feet of space in an arcade or store. That's not much. The game uses very little electricity. And it doesn't break down very often. An average game in an average location will take in from $200 to $800 a week. That means in a few months the game can make back its initial cost. A good machine, in a good location, can take in as much as $2,000 a week in quarters. It can pay for itself in two weeks. After that it's all profit.

Manufacturers generally sell their machines to distributors. The distributors then lease the machines to arcades, stores, movie theaters or wherever. Usually the distributor then takes half of what the machine pulls in. The other half goes to the owner of the place where it is located. On a popular game the profits mount up fast.

Every new game seems to do well at first. Everyone wants to try the latest challenge. But many of the games don't have any staying power. Even a moderately successful game lasts only six months to a year. Then it's off to the scrap heap. The superstars of the arcades, game like Space Invaders and Asteroids, are still pulling in quarters years after they were

introduced. But gradually they, too, will fade away, because they are no longer being manufactured. In fact, except for the game superstars, a three-month manufacturing run is considered good. When a game is at the height of popularity in the arcades, it is already on its way out for the manufacturer.

36

We've all heard about the winners; what about the flops?

"There are lots of flops," says *Electronic Games* editor Bill Kunkel. "There's Shark Attack, where you control the shark and the chomp button. Bite the diver and there are spurts of color that turn the water blood red.

"Another one shows a burning orphanage that has firemen holding nets trying to catch children jumping out of the building. If they miss the kid goes splat, then turns into an angel and floats off the screen and you don't get any points. Those are cute graphics, but I wonder if the makers have given any thought to what they are doing. That's sick."

As soon as a game is successful, other manufacturers try to imitate it. No one tries to imitate the flops. After the success of Space Invaders the arcades were filled with that type of game. Asteroids has its imitators. So does Pac-Man. If the imitations get too close, the manufacturers sue. Sometimes they win the lawsuits, sometimes they don't. The lawyers have made a bundle out of video games, too. Usually, though, an imitation game can be made just different enough to be legal.

It only takes about eight weeks to get a new machine out on the street. For that reason the makers of a hot new game guard their secrets closely. They don't want a competitor out with an imitation of their new hit before they get a solid lock on the market. At moments the fun world of video games seems a bit like the grim world of international spying.

The publications of the video game industry regularly list the most popular games. Those involved in making and selling the machines check the popularity charts as closely as people in the record industry check the charts of the top record sellers, booksellers check the best-seller list or movie makers check the list of the most profitable movies.

What's hot right now? It's hard to say because the list changes all the time. By the time you read this it has undoubtedly changed again. But here is what the top ten in the arcade games were in the early summer of 1982 according to the magazine *Electronic Games*.

Number one was, of course, Pac-Man, the long-time favorite, which seemed to keep gobbling right along, despite rumors of its imminent fall from popularity.

After that came Tempest, Defender, Asteroids (another long-time favorite), Centipede, Battlezone, Berzerk, Crazy Climber, Wizard of Wor and Donkey Kong.

Most arcade games are upright consoles—a rectangular box with a TV screen in it. But many popular games also appear in table form. The screen is set into the top of the table, and the player can sit rather than stand. The table-type of game is most common in restaurants and bars. They are rarely found in arcades. The true arcader stands up to play.

If you like to show off, the video arcade is a good place to do it. In most games your score is right out there for everybody to see while you are playing. If you get the high score for the day or for that particular machine, you can record your initials or name and it will be flashed on the screen for all to see—until someone else beats your score.

In 1981 *Omni* magazine ran an unconfirmed rumor contest. One of the runners-up in the contest was Larry Pike of Portland, Oregon. The rumor that he either heard or made up was this:

"Popular arcade games such as Asteroids, Space Invaders and Tail Gunner are programmed to record the initials of the highest-scoring player. When you enter your initials, a photograph is secretly taken of you. The 'games' are actually mechanisms for selecting, sorting and training slave labor for duty in military spacecraft and star bases. People who get good at these machines disappear under suspicious circumstances. You won't find *my* initials on one of those things no matter how good I get!"

You won't find *my* initials there, either, because I'll never get that good. The rumor, of course, is completely silly, but you might try it out on a few of your friends. Who knows, it could worry them a bit and lower their scores. Then you may be able to beat them.

In most arcade games you don't ever really win. There is no jackpot at the end. But there is no time limit, either. The better you are the higher your score and the longer you can play on a single quarter. If you get really good you might be able to play half an hour or more on a single quarter—a good bargain.

The real video game wizards try to set records by piling up the largest number of points and playing the longest time on a quarter. Local papers are always carrying stories about this or that kid who managed to keep playing Asteroids or Pac-Man for ten or twelve hours until the machine broke. Such wonders are rare, but they do happen. And that brings up a question. During these marathon sessions, when does the player eat, when does he go to the bathroom?

That depends on the player's endurance. And it depends on the game he is playing. In some games the player can build up scoring reserves and so be able to get away briefly without losing the game. Other games contain small programming flaws that allow the player to find a safe spot to rest. The flaws are less common and harder to take advantage of than arcade rumor would have it.

The makers of arcade games have to walk a

Atari® Space Duel™

thin line. The game has to be easy enough so
that people can learn to play it quickly. If it is
too complicated people will become dis-
couraged and give up. But the game can't be so
easy that it can be played for hours on a
quarter. There is obviously no profit in such a
game. Besides, arcaders want a challenge, not
a pushover.

A major drawback for most arcade games is
the instructions. The instructions for almost all
the games are pretty scanty. It takes even
experienced gamers a couple of dollars before
they learn to play adequately. The best thing to
do with a new game is watch someone else play
it first. Don't depend on the instructions alone.

How long before you become an expert—the
kind of player who draws a crowd at an arcade? That depends on you, your reflexes,
coordination, memory and dedication. And it
depends on the game—some are lots harder
than others. Most experienced arcade watch-
ers agree that it takes at least $40 or $50 in
quarters to become good at any new game.

The great success of Space Invaders and
Asteroids left the general impression that all
arcade games were warlike. The object was to
zap the enemy—to destroy his spaceships before he destroyed you. For a while the vast
majority of arcade video games were of the
"zap" type. Many still are. But the image of

the arcade game is changing. The most popular arcade game of our time, Pac-Man, is a maze game, and so are the many Pac-Man imitators.

Sports games have always had their fans. But they have never become a major part of the video arcade scene.

Driving games, on the other hand, have always had a place in the video game arcade. In these the player uses fairly realistic controls to guide his vehicle through a series of obstacles. No driving game has ever become an arcade superstar of the magnitude of Pac-Man, but they have a regular core of supporters who keep feeding them quarters. That encourages manufacturers to develop new and even more sophisticated driving games.

A brilliant example of this new type of driving game is Sega/Gremlin's Turbo. Turbo comes in two sizes: the familiar upright console, and a cockpit type. In the cockpit the player sits down in front of the controls just as he would in a real race car. Controls consist of a steering wheel, gearshift and a gas pedal. But what's best about the game are the graphics. The scene changes from day to night, from city to tree-lined highway to a dangerous oceanside curve. There are tunnels and twisting or ice-covered roads. All in all, a challenging and remarkably realistic experience.

And speaking of graphics, there is a whole

class of games that depend mainly on their graphics for popularity, and their popularity has been increasing. These have been dubbed the cartoon games. The class includes such favorites as Donkey Kong (Donkey is a rough translation of the Japanese word for stupid), Crazy Climber, Frogger and Bally's new Kick Man. A bonus for Kick Man is that it includes a guest appearance by the ever popular Pac-Man. That is perhaps the first guest shot for a famous video game character. But it won't be the last.

For sheer graphic brilliance you can't beat Zaxxon, another Sega/Gremlin product. It's a mixture of driving and zap game. You maneuver your ship into a fortress while fighting off enemy ships and confronting the ultimate weapon, the missile-firing enemy robot. The graphics have an incredible three-dimensional realism. Comparing the graphics of a game like Zaxxon to those of an old classic like Space Invaders is a bit like comparing stick figures to Rembrandt. The sounds, too, have progressed way beyond the buzzers and bongs of the early games. The games really talk to you now.

Greater realism and imagination in graphics is where the arcade games appear to be headed.

# CHAPTER 5

# THERE'S NO PLACE LIKE HOME

Why home video? Why not keep feeding your quarters into the arcade games? After all, the arcade games are more spectacular and offer you more of a challenge. If you're good, you'll shine like a star. You'll collect a crowd of admirers around you. It's harder to be a hero at home.

But wait a minute. What if you don't like crowds? What if you'd rather be by yourself or with a small group of friends? Maybe you're happier at home than hanging out in an arcade. And what if you don't have an endless supply of quarters? Besides, how do you get to be good at anything except by practicing? Once you've bought your home video cartridge you can practice as much as you want without having to worry about who's looking at you and without caring about whether you've got any more quarters. In home video the more you use your cartridges the more you get your money's worth out of them. So play it again, Sam.

Okay, you're sold. You're ready to buy a home video system. So you go down to a department store or a discount store and the confusion sets in. I remember when I used to go shopping with a friend who was a stereo freak. He was always looking for this new gadget or that new component. When he tried to help me put together my first stereo system I thought I'd go crazy. I didn't know where to begin.

So let's you and I talk about how to begin. Once you get past the hype, the jargon and the complexities of computer technology it's really very simple. The three major home video game systems are Atari, Mattel, and Magnavox/Odyssey. A new contender, Coleco, is making its appearance. If you shop at Sears you can buy a variation of either Atari or Intellivision with a selection of cartridges from either of those companies and special cartridges made strictly for Sears.

Atari, Mattel and Odyssey all have a lot in common. They offer a wide variety of well-designed games with good graphics. You can't really go wrong with any of them. Still, they

have their differences. The system that works
for one person might be disappointing to another. So before you make your purchase ask
yourself what kind of person you are.

Atari is the giant of the field. They make the
most cartridges. There are now some seventy
Atari game cartridges. Other companies make
cartridges compatible with Atari, but Odyssey
does not. Odyssey's cartridges are for Odyssey. Imagic makes cartridges compatible with
Odyssey and Atari. So, nice as it would be if
there were a home video system that took
every new game cartridge, you just don't have

that choice. There are new software companies entering the field all the time. The confusion will get worse.

Let's get back to Atari. Besides variety, what else does it have to offer? Well, Atari has Space Invaders and Asteroids, two great video game classics. Its position as a leader in space games is secure. And Atari is uniquely suited to adapt arcade games for home video because Atari is a major manufacturer of arcade games.

Atari's games are generally exciting and less complex than Mattel's. The controls have been criticized, but then I have heard and read criticisms of the controls on all the systems. The Atari paddle controllers are more responsive than the joystick. But they are used less often. You can always buy an improved or specialized controller if you want. For example, Atari sells a driving controller that can be used in place of the joystick in their racing games.

Atari has developed the Atari Supergame system, which will feature more advanced games with highly sophisticated graphics. The Supergame system is not meant to replace the standard Atari VCS (video computer system). There will be plenty of new cartridges for the popular model so many kids already own.

On to Mattel's Intellivision—Intelligent Television, as they like to describe themselves. The Mattel system uses hand controls with buttons and a disc. Some people find that it takes longer to learn how to use these controls than the Atari controls but that once learned they provide great flexibility. Mattel is famous for its graphics. The pictures you'll see on your television are really beautiful and often very realistic. Though noted mainly for its sports action games, Intellivision has a line of space

# Intellivision® Cartridges
## New for 1982

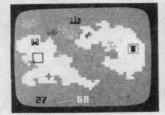

Utopia™

Pinball
(working name only)

Star Strike™

Tron I**
(working name only)

Card Fun
(working name only)

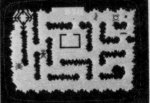

Night Stalker™

Advanced
Dungeons & Dragons™

Sub Hunt™

Tron II**
(working name only)

Space Hawk™

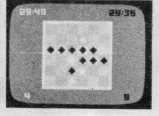

action games, and as a master coup will present the home video version of Tron, based on the Walt Disney movie. Basketball II is a spectacular new sports game on its way.

Mattel also offers strategy games like Chess and learning games like Math Fun. And their prize fantasy adventure game is an advanced Dungeons and Dragons cartridge. If that isn't enough for you, Mattel is introducing Intellivoice. This is a brand new kind of module that allows you to plug in a special unit that actually talks to you. Yes, I mean it, it talks to you.

**VOICE CARTRIDGES**

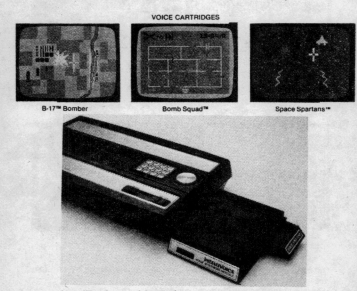

B-17™ Bomber          Bomb Squad™          Space Spartans™

Intellivoice™, Mattel's voice synthesis module

As you play you will hear a voice react to the game, give you advice and, in general, try to enhance the fun. This is certainly a big breakthrough in home video games. Intellivoice can first be heard on cartridges such as Space Spartans, B-17 Bombers and Bomb Squad.

So consider Intellivision if you're patient and like a game that's challenging but slower than Atari. If you are especially interested in sports games, Mattel's Intellivision may be for you.

To show you why, let's zoom in on one of Mattel's best games, Major League Baseball, which has been listed in the *Electronic Games* magazine Hall of Fame. There are a variety of pitches. The batter can even bunt. The running game is beautifully detailed. And when there is a good play you hear the roar of the crowd.

On to Odyssey. In 1972 Magnavox introduced the first home video game called Odyssey. It was extremely simple and primitive, naturally. In honor of this first game the entire system born from it has been christened Odyssey, or to be more precise, Odyssey II.

Odyssey has had a lot of experience, and here's what you get for it. The controls of the new Odyssey II system consist of both a keyboard unit and joysticks. You won't have to buy a lot of extra gadgetry. So you have both a simple and complex system combined for no extra cost. One cartridge, Keyboard Creations, allows you to create your own word and number games.

Odyssey has fewer cartridges than either Mattel or Atari. But what they have is excellent and imaginative. Two of the best of the new ones are Monkeyshines, where the little

CHALLENGER SERIES

**MONKEYSHINES!**
Computerized monkeys! Unlimited action!!
*Trillions* of combinations!!! You'll go ape!!!!

Odyssey voice module

apes swing, jump and climb across endless monkey bars, and U.F.O. You must free space from the dastardly Empire's blockade of Starduster Drone Mines and hunter-killer Fireball Satellites. The game also includes a display of the high score and player's name. That's common in the arcade but new to home video. Odyssey is also offering a voice module called "Voice of Odyssey." Among other things it will allow the user to play spelling games.

If you like fantasy games, Odyssey's are especially exciting. Their triumph is the famous Quest for the Rings, another game in *Electronic Games* magazine's Hall of Fame. Ten rings of power lie hidden within the Dark Lands of the evil Ringmaster. Firewraths,

Bloodthirsts and Dragons guard the rings. The game has heroes and wizards and has blended the elements of both board and video games. What's more, instead of competing, the human players must cooperate in collecting the rings. The graphics are super and the game is not needlessly complex. You can learn it and play it quickly. So don't overlook Odyssey when you do your shopping.

There is one more system, a brand new one called ColecoVision™, a product of Coleco

Industries, Inc. In addition to its own system, Coleco has started manufacturing cartridges that can be used with Atari and Mattel. These include the great arcade game Donkey Kong, the spectacular Zaxxon and the zany, lovable Smurf. This game is based on the blue stars of the hit Saturday morning television show.

Coleco's full system will introduce a very precise game controller. Players will be able to change speed during actual game play or stop action altogether. A really super bonus is an expansion module (available separately) that allows you to use Atari software (cartridges). So check out ColecoVision™.

2400 ColecoVision™
Video Game System

When choosing your video game system don't forget to check the price of the various units. Some, like Mattel and Coleco, cost more than others. You may feel it's worth it to spend more, but certainly price is something you must keep in mind.

You've bought it and you're home hooking the system up to your television. You feel like you're surrounded by black spaghetti. Untwisting wires is one of the negative sides of playing home video games. The tangle of wires is a distinct drawback to all home video systems. Hopefully future technology will correct the difficulty.

Let's say you have an Atari VCS. Most kids do. The game found most frequently in American homes is Combat because it comes with the Atari.

Most Atari games have several skill levels. You can generally practice at an easy level and work your way up. Atari's graphics tend to be abstract and are often beautiful. For instance, look at Yars' Revenge, a space game where the good guys are mutant flies. Your video screen literally shimmers. It's as if you are in space. Even the sound has caught that.

Recently I conducted an extremely unscientific test. I asked the neighborhood kids what their favorite games were. A lot said Breakout. If you think breaking through a brick wall was exciting, wait till you see SuperBreakout. The new game glows with color. But even the color is secondary to the clear ring of musical notes—you'll feel like a composer. By the way, if you're a circus fan, Atari has a game called Circus where clowns bounce upward (score) or downward (splat) from a seesaw. Knocking the ball around in SuperBreakout requires similar maneuvers.

Atari used good sound effects right from the beginning. Listen to the ominous tramping noises of Space Invaders, still one of the all-time masterpieces among video games. But to see how quickly home video games have changed, try Warlords. The video screen is filled with action and the possibilities of play have increased. And wait till you see Demons. Here, the targets can actually be transformed into menacing enemies by your own mistakes. It's an exciting, quick-moving game, a true advance on your ordinary shooting gallery.

Right now might be a good place to point out that Atari has games in every imaginable category. Like home video variations of arcade games. Atari not only has Pac-Man but is also introducing the popular Berserk. So if this nutty game with Evil Otto giving chase is your kind of fun, Atari has it. At home Otto has, alas, lost his voice. Want howling winds, ghosts and a search through a haunted mansion? Play Haunted House. It's not the easiest game to learn, but if you don't mind putting out a little effort it's worth it.

If you go for classic games, the type that in pre-video games were played only on boards, Atari offers you Othello, Checkers, 3-D Tic-Tac-Toe, Chess and Backgammon. Want a gambling game? Try Casino. There's a whole range of driving games, each with a different set of challenges. You can race down a hill or against a clock, follow a winding road at night where obstacles come at you from nowhere or get smashed to smithereens in Dodge Em.

Combat games your specialty? You can blast away at enemies, pretend you're in a shooting gallery, drop make-believe bombs into a canyon, be a gunfighter in the wild West. Sports fans will like Basketball, Football, Golf and Pelé's Soccer. If you enjoy practicing your pitching and batting, there's Homerun.

For a change of style try Brain Games and see how good your memory is. How are you at breaking secret codes? Take a crack at a video version of the old standby word game, Hangman. Remember, you don't have to play one kind of game all the time. You don't have to be a sports fan to play sports video games. And even if you're the top hitter on your school baseball team you might find that when it comes to video games you'd rather play Concentration. Though the things we like to do often affect our choice of video games, it's silly to be too rigid. And obviously a company like Atari that makes so many games is bound to come up with an occasional dud. Still, to make full use of computer home video games you have to be open to a wide range of imaginative possibilities.

No Atari collection is complete unless it has a good sprinkling of software made by other companies for Atari. Parker Brothers, the company that makes some of the finest board games in the world, including the great classic Monopoly®, has begun producing software compatible with Atari VCS. Starting with The Empire Strikes Back™ cartridge they are developing a line of games based on *Star Wars*. The Empire Strikes Back cartridge has Imperial Walkers attacking the Rebel base on the Ice Planet Hoth. This game should appeal to all you *Star Wars* fans. And practically everybody's heard of the Sega/Gremlin arcade game Frogger™. Thanks to Parker Brothers, Frogger will now leap across your video screen, first dodging traffic, then dodging deadly crocodiles as he tries to make it across a rushing river.

If you want my vote on what is one of the best video games, I'd say Activision's Kaboom. If you don't already know the Mad Bomber, you might think about making his acquaintance. You try to catch the bombs he drops, but when your last bucket of water misses, wham, he's got you. And he grins to prove it. If you score above 10,000 you will wipe the grin off his face. In the chapter on Pac-Man I said that Pac-Man was a great cartoon creation. Well, so is the Mad Bomber. Part of what makes this game engaging is his personality. You'll be seeing a lot more of this sort of approach in home video games.

But I must confess I find Activision an especially innovative and imaginative company. For example, I can tell you that Larry Kaplan designed Kaboom. It's much harder to find out who designs Atari games. And although other companies have fan clubs, Activision really goes out of its way to keep its followers informed. If you're really good at a game you can join one of the Activision clubs. Just send a photo of your TV screen showing your score. If eligible you'll get a patch or certificate. And through the company's newsletter, *Activision,* you'll find out the names of the champion scorers.

Atari games usually have more levels of play than Activision games, but Activision more than compensates for this by the clever use of graphics and design. Take Freeway. It's an update on the old story about the chicken crossing the road. Starting with Chicago's

Outer Drive and moving on to other highways at busier times of day you try to guide the fluttering white bird to safety. It gets knocked around quite a bit in the process. What you hear through all this is the astonishingly realistic noise of traffic.

If you like sports games, Activision offers Ice Hockey, Skiing, Fishing Derby, Boxing and Tennis. My favorite is Tennis, maybe because the controls work extremely well, maybe because I like to watch "the pro" dash madly around the court and maybe because the players are not just dull shapes on the screen as in so many sports games but look like real tennis players. It is scored like the real game and you can play it against the computer, "the pro" or with a friend. It's very challenging. It's also cute, right down to the shadow under the tennis ball.

Like driving games? Try Dragster and Grand Prix. In Grand Prix you aim for speed. You have a choice of race courses, and if you pace yourself and practice you'll be hypnotized by the game before you know it. Like a lot of other Activision games girls as well as boys like Grand Prix, Dragster and Freeway. Activision games are exciting but not macho, with a strong emphasis on attractive visual effects.

If you want strategy games they offer Bridge and Checkers. And in the space game category they have Laser Blast. It's a get-them-before-they-get-you sort of game calling for good timing. You'll love the color. A more complicated space game, StarMaster, is new from Activision. This one's complete with meteor showers and enemy particle cannons. You're piloting a spacecraft under attack and must rely on computer readouts for information to make decisions.

A popular new space game is Megamania. You not only have to shoot down enemy ships, you also have to conserve your own power supply.

Their new combat game is Chopper Command. You're flying escort for a truck convoy of medical supplies when enemy aircraft appear. You have laser rockets. They have multi-warhead missiles.

Around our house the favorite Activision games are Stampede and Barnstorming. What's interesting about Stampede is that it requires you to do several different things at once. Not only must you lasso running cattle while riding a horse but you must also keep your eye on the whole herd at once. Otherwise you'll let a few get behind you and you lose points on the game. As if that isn't enough to worry about, every once in a while you'll see a black Angus bull. He's hardest of all to get because he's sitting still. And there's this skull you keep tripping over.

A new game is Pitfall!, a game with super
graphics. The player must guide a traveler
through a danger-filled jungle adventure in
twenty minutes or less.

Barnstorming's appeal is a little bit like Kaboom's. It has charm. Simply put, your little
biplane must rise above towers and swoop
through barns. Now come the touches that
make Barnstorming clever. When the plane
hits the towers it really hits. You'll shudder
along with the plane and you'll laugh. Or bang
up against a barn. Boink! And, of course, there
are the geese. Let's see if you can avoid them,
noisy little beasts.

Activision has just started making cartridges for Intellivision. The first two are Pitfall! and the new Stampede, both also available in Atari-compatible cartridges.

Okay, you say, all the games in this chapter sound great. But you haven't got all the money in the world. How do you make your choices? The best way is to find a store that will let you try the games out. Some will. Some won't. You'll have to ask around. Another good way is to borrow games from a friend. If you like a game you'll probably want to buy it sooner or later. But at least you'll know what you're getting before you spend any money. It might be worth your while to invest in a game program case to hold your cartridges and keep them in good condition. After all, the games aren't cheap.

So use some judgment. Try to zoom in on the types of games you like. Then read the manufacturers' descriptions of the games. You ought to get a feel for what is your kind of challenge.

But don't be so practical you pass up new adventures. The home video market is booming and the games are likely to get better every year.

Have fun!

# Chapter 6

# The Games Computers Play

Everybody knows about the arcade video games. If you are reading this book you certainly own or have played some home video games, too. But there is another type of video game, one that you may not be familiar with yet. And it may have the brightest future of all. It is the computer game.

"Hold on," you say. "A while back you told us that all video games are computer games." Well, yes, I did say that. And now I'm going to take part of it back. The arcade games and the home video games use very simple computers. These game computers are good for only one thing—playing games. The kind of computer games that we will be talking about in this chapter are played on computers that can be used for lots of other things. I suppose you could say they are played on "real" computers.

In order to play one of these computer games you have to have a computer. An expensive home video game system will cost a couple of hundred dollars. A good home computer will cost several thousand dollars. And then you have to know how to use the computer. That can take time. Simpler and cheaper systems are now becoming available.

The chances are that you have never played a real computer game. You may never have even seen anyone play such a game. But more and more people are buying home computers. One day they may be as common in the home as TV sets are today. These computers can be used for a lot of things: homework, figuring income tax and playing games. More and more schools are offering courses in computers to their students. Computers are part of the future—your future. So let's take a look at some of the games that can be played on computers right now. Even if you can't play them yet, you may be able to very soon.

Many home computers come with their own video display screen—their own TV set. But you can't get HBO or anything else on the screen. It is strictly for computer use. The guts of the computer are in a box, bigger than the home video game console. It has a keyboard, and the user types in information and questions. The keyboard can also be used for game playing. However, computers can be fitted out with joysticks or paddles for game playing.

Many game programs are available for home computers. The programs or software come on disks or tape casettes. Some of these programs are produced by companies that make other types of video games, like Atari. Atari also makes home computers. There are many other home computer companies. Not all software can be used with all computers. The computer owner has to be careful in buying programs.

The computer has a larger memory and can simply do more things than a home video game. While there are programs for arcade-style action games, the computer doesn't really do them as well as they can be done in the arcade. But the games are still good. And there are types of games that can be played on the computer that will never be seen in the arcades.

OK, cut the theory, let's get practical and look at some of the games. We'll start with something familiar. It's called Jawbreaker. *Electronic Games* magazine named it the best computer action game of 1981.

The player has to maneuver a set of chomping teeth through a candy-filled maze. The teeth accumulate points by wolfing down round candies and assorted other goodies. The teeth are chased through the maze by a quartet of round-faced bullies. Actually, they are just round faces that smile when they are winning. If the bullies catch the teeth, the teeth have had it. But when the teeth chomp up a jawbreaker, one of the candies in the maze, then the bullies start frowning and turn blue. For a brief period the teeth can gobble up the bullies. That adds extra points to the score. The bullies' ghosts fly back to the center of the maze. They reemerge as new bullies and the chase begins again.

Does all of that sound a bit familiar? Sure it does. Jawbreaker is clearly patterned after the ever popular Pac-Man. But the graphics are really much better than those of the home video version of Pac-Man. The game has more variations, too. And when it starts you are treated to an electronic rendition of "The Candy Man."

Another familiar type of game is County Fair. It is basically an electronic shooting gallery. The player uses a joystick to move a pistol back and forth. He fires electronic bullets at ducks, rabbits and other targets.

All familiar enough, so far. But the computer has the capacity to allow for a couple of nice little extra touches. When they are shot, the duck targets fall to the bottom of the screen.

Sometimes they will get up and eat the player's extra ammunition. The rabbit targets multiply before your very eyes. If you get all of the stationary targets you then have to shoot a flying duck. And after completely clearing the screen you have to start over again. But this time the targets move more quickly.

The same type of game played on a home video game system is much more limited. The simple home video system would have no capacity to produce bullet-gobbling ducks.

Sports games are not a major part of the computer game field. At least not yet. Of the sports games the best are baseball simulations. Perhaps that is because most baseball freaks are also statistics freaks. Statistics are what computers handle best.

*Electronic Games* magazine picked the aptly named Computer Baseball as the best computer sports game for 1981.

The game is designed for two people. Each becomes the manager of a famous world series team. The names of the actual players on the team are flashed on the screen. The "managers" pick their lineups and play begins. Each baseball player's individual strengths and weaknesses are taken into account. The "managers" call all the shots. But this is not an action game. The game player does not press a button to "hit" the ball.

Drawing on its vast store of information on the performances of the particular baseball players, the computer decides whether the player makes a hit or an out. If the player at bat is a good hitter he is more likely to make a hit. Will a fielder handle a ball cleanly, or will he boot it? That will depend on the fielder's past record with the glove.

As the game wears on the starting pitchers begin to "tire." They are less effective. Sometimes they must be taken out. As in real baseball, the manager can't just stick in a reliever. The relief pitcher has to have a chance to warm up. But if he warms up too long he will leave his good stuff in the bullpen. All the decisions a real major-league manager makes during a game are made by the players of Computer Baseball.

There is also a one-player version of the game. In that the computer takes the place of the opposing manager. The computer manager is called Casey, naturally.

The problem is the graphics. They aren't that great. You can see the ball being pitched, hit and fielded—but it is more diagrammatic than exciting. Computer Baseball, and most computer sports games, are more intellectual tests and tests of knowledge than they are action games. Reflexes and hand–eye coordination are irrelevant to most of these games.

There is an area of game playing in which the computer really excels—the fantasy adventure game. Such games barely exist in the arcades or regular home video games. (Odyssey's Quest For The Rings is the notable exception.) Most of these fantasy adventure games appear to have been inspired in one way or another by the game Dungeons and Dragons. The player takes the role of some fantasy character. Then the gamester has to make his or her way through a place filled with dangers or complete a certain number of tasks. There is a final goal in the adventure. It can be capturing an object, overthrowing a super villain or just getting out of a place alive. Along the way the gamester can pick up aid, like a magic sword, or he can incur liabilities, a wound, for example.

Like Dungeons and Dragons, most of the adventure games have a heroic fantasy background. But not all of them do. The *Electronic Games* 1981 pick for outstanding computer adventure game was Empire of the Over-Mind. It had more of a science fiction, *Star Wars* setting. The hero has to battle the evil overmind, who has enslaved twin worlds. There are several different ways in which overthrowing the over-mind can be accomplished—and many more ways to fail.

Wow, you think, what kind of graphics do they use for that? The very disappointing answer is, none. It's what's called a text adventure. The situation in which the hero finds him or herself is described on the screen in words. The player punches in a response on the keyboard—a couple of words. The computer then responds with some more words that explain the new situation confronting the hero. It's like a short story written in collaboration with a computer.

D & D players can probably relate to this kind of a game more easily than veteran arcaders. The D & D player doesn't need pictures. Dungeons and Dragons is a game of imagination. The computer can take the place of the dungeonmaster who makes up the rules. But for those who love zapping aliens with the press of an action button, such a game may seem dull—not really a video game at all.

Well, to each his or her own. But don't dismiss the fantasy adventure game out of hand. Graphics are coming. There are programs now available for illustrated adventures. Some of the words are replaced by figures which have limited movement. It is an illustrated text. The words are still most important. In other programs some of the maneuvers and fights are controlled by a joystick. As the newer programs are produced the graphics are becoming more and more elaborate and more and more important. They still have a long way to go. But they have already come a long way in a short time.

In mid-1982 computer gamesters were enthusiastic over an adventure game with a different setting. It is called Castle Wolfenstein. The object is to get a captured Allied war prisoner out of a Nazi fortress called Castle Wolfenstein. The castle has sixty rooms and is prowled by SS guards, who actually speak German, or at least bark out a few commands in German. The screen shows the plans of the castle and the movements of the guards. The player must either outshoot the guards, hide from them or lock the door against them—if he can find the key. Some guards carry keys or weapons, or their uniforms can be taken as a disguise. Each time the game is played the arrangement of the castle is different. And the guards are in different places. Every time a prisoner succeeds in escaping—that is, the player wins the game—he is given a higher rank. That means next time the game is harder.

It's all there—the sounds, the graphics, the action and the adventure. And it can only get better in the future.

There is another thing you can look forward to with computers. You may be able to program your own games. That is certainly something you can't do in the arcade.

# CHAPTER 7

# THE GREAT VIDEO GAME CONTROVERSY

There are people who hate video games. They think the games are a danger to the young people of America. It's hard to believe that there is anyone in the world who could hate Pac-Man. But it's true.

Some cities and towns have tried to limit video games. Others have tried to ban them completely. Many video game cases are now in the courts. Educators and parents' groups have spoken out against video games. All sorts of politicians have become involved in the controversy.

To the average arcader happily pouring his quarters into a machine, or to the home player, the whole dispute is a puzzle. What's behind it?

There are lots of things. The roots of this controversy go back a long way.

A large part of the problem comes from the fact that video games first made it big in the arcades. Arcades have never had a particularly good reputation in America. Arcades were places where kids were supposed to hang around wasting time and money.

All coin-operated games are suspected of being gambling machines. One of the best known of all coin-op machines is the slot machine—the well-named one-armed bandit. The slot machine is a gambling machine, nothing more or less. It is strictly a game of chance. In most places slot machines are illegal. Legal slot machines are allowed only in places that allow gambling—Las Vegas, Atlantic City and the like. Kids are not allowed in gambling casinos. Illegal slot machines are found in a lot of very respectable private clubs, however. People just don't like to talk about them.

When the pinball machine was first introduced it, too, was a gambling machine. It didn't have any flippers. The score you got was pure chance. If you got a high score there was a payoff, in cash. It wasn't big-time gambling, but it was gambling.

New York City's colorful Mayor Fiorello La Guardia went on the offensive against the pinball machine. He called it a "perverter of innocent children." He went after the machines with sledge hammer and the law. He succeeded in having the machines banned in the city. Other large cities, like Chicago and Los Angeles, also banned pinball machines.

The pinball machine industry responded by changing the machine. The flippers were put in. That made the machine more of a game of skill than a game of pure chance. All the machines were labeled "For Amusement Only." The arcades and other places where the games were played stopped paying off. By the 1950s the pinball machine really had become a game "For Amusement Only." But its past history as a gambling machine still clung to it.

When the video game moved into the arcades and took over from the pinball machine, it also took over some of the pinball machine's bad reputation. The video game, however, is not a gambling device. The video game arcade is not a gambling casino, though some people seem to think it is. Video versions of blackjack and poker can be found in some casinos, but not in arcades.

The video game has created some of its own special problems. No one ever accused the pinball machine of being violent. That is one of the charges leveled most frequently against video games.

That problem did not start immediately. No

one called Pong violent. Some of the early tank battles and shootout games passed unnoticed. Then there was an early game called Death Race. It attracted a lot of hostile attention.

Basically Death Race was a driving game. As in most driving games the object was to stay on the road. In most driving games you have to avoid obstacles. In Death Race the point was to hit them. The obstacles were little "gremlins" that dashed across the road. If the player hit one he scored points. Each time a "gremlin" was hit a tombstone appeared in its place. The driver then had to avoid hitting the tombstones. The graphics were clever. The idea behind the game was not.

The manufacturers of Death Race called it good, clean fun. Others said it was sick, or an invitation to reckless hit-and-run driving. The controversy over video games had begun in earnest.

The image of video games as too violent was not helped by Space Invaders and all the Space Invader imitations. While it wasn't quite like Death Race, you still scored points by "killing" something. In Asteriods the "enemy" was more abstract. It was a hunk of rock or a spaceship. But once again, something had to be shot and blown up. Thus the picture of the arcade as a place that encouraged violence among the young was strengthened. Never mind the fact that there were also sports games and driving games that were not at all like Death Race. Those were not the games that dominated the arcades.

And then came Pac-Man. Admittedly Packy is regularly "destroyed." And he does gobble up the monsters when given half a chance. But it's not a violent game. Nor are a score of other Pac-Man imitators. They are maze games.

Cartoon games like Crazy Climber, Donkey Kong and Frogger may have an implied violence. Poor climbing Mario in Donkey Kong may get bopped with a barrel. The unfortunate frog may get squashed or chomped up by a crocodile. But the graphics are so funny that it is hard for anyone to get upset. Besides, the aim of the game is to avoid violence, not to create it. The arcader picks up points when Mario jumps the barrel or the frog gets away from the crocodile.

Most arcades are still dominated by zap games of one sort or the other. But that image is changing, and it's changing fast. It can no longer be said that all arcade video games encourage violence.

As we have seen, the arcade itself had an image problem. It seemed a bit like the pool hall. In the early days of video games the only people who spent much time around arcades were teenaged boys. Pac-Man brought in the girls. The cartoon games are bringing in younger children. Some arcades are really starting to be what arcades have always pretended to be, true family entertainment centers. While there are still many sleazy arcades, there are also many very good ones.

There is no better example of the coin-op arcade's changing image than the Tomorrowland Starcade in Disneyland. No one has ever accused the Magic Kingdom of sleaziness. The Tomorrowland Starcade has all the favorite arcade games, often in giant-sized or sit-in models. If it is as successful as it now appears to be, the Starcade will set the style and the tone for arcades all over the country. The Disney movie *Tron* and its video game tie-in will undoubtedly encourage further cooperation between the Disney organization and the video game industry.

But the problem for the arcade games is not image alone. They do present some real problems. One of the most common complaints leveled against the games is that kids spend their lunch money on them. The games can cost a lot of money. Five or six dollars in quarters can disappear in no time. One California arcade owner boasted that when the kids left his place they didn't have any money left to spend on dope!

Clearly anyone who is spending more money

than he or she can afford on video games has got a problem.

The time spent playing the games is another problem. There have been a lot of complaints that kids spend too much time on Asteroids and Pac-Man. There are stories about kids skipping school to hang out at arcades. Or not doing their homework because they spend too much time playing games. Or coming home from arcades late at night. That, too, can be a real problem.

Some people object to arcades because they tend to be noisy places and crowds of teenagers collect in and around them. Still another objection is to the sheer number of machines. At times it seems as if every single store in the neighborhood has at least one, and usually several, of the video quarter gulpers.

There have also been scarier rumors. The games are said to be "hypnotic" and "addictive." In truth, there is no evidence that the games are any more "hypnotic" or "addictive" than other forms of entertainment. People have been "hypnotized" by television. They become "addicted" to playing cards. There are even times when people sit up too late reading a good book. Video games are no different. They have no special powers to turn your brain to oatmeal.

The same sort of charges were regularly

raised against any new development in the field of entertainment—movies, radio, electronically amplified music and television. People who were denounced for listening to rock music and watching too much television when they were young now turn around and denounce the young for spending time playing video games. It's always been that way. Somehow it seems that things were always better when we were young—whenever that might have been.

Some have reacted so violently against the games you have to wonder if something else isn't going on. It may be unfamiliarity and discomfort with the new technology the games represent that frightens people so badly. Since most people don't understand how the games work, they tend to regard them as evil, dangerous and far more powerful than they really are. Young people, on the other hand, accept the games and simply enjoy them.

Home video games have never received the sort of criticism that has plagued the arcade games. At home the very same games seem to be thought of as simple entertainment. Perhaps as older people become more familiar with video games, they will be less fearful of them.

In the Philippines video games have been banned entirely. The government said they were supposed to be bad for the youth of the nation. It was an odd bit of morality in a nation ruled by a dictator and noted for having some of the seamiest night life in the world.

Various communities in America have also attempted to ban video games. Sometimes they want to close down a particular arcade. At other times they want to get rid of the games no matter where they are. The owners of the arcades, and the manufacturers of games, which are, after all, extremely profitable, are usually willing to fight the bans in court. Total bans on video games have proved difficult to enforce.

Cities and towns have been more successful in trying to restrict the hours of arcades, or to set limits on the age of those who can enter the arcades without their parents.

Most of those in the video game business either believe that the objections to the games are trivial or would simply rather not talk about the problems.

Others insist that the games are not merely an enjoyable pastime but a positive influence. They teach a certain amount of hand–eye coordination, but far more significantly they familiarize young people with the world of computers and electronics, which will be such an important part of their lives in the future.

Video games are still relatively new in our

society. They have hit with an impact that practically no one expected. It will take a while before we learn to deal with them in a sensible way. In the meantime kids should realize they can't spend all their time and money on the games. And older folks should relax. The games are not going to turn the young into a generation of zombies.

# CHAPTER 8

# VIDEO GAMES WITHOUT VIDEO

Since electronics has invaded the game field there has been a lot of confusion. Sometimes nonvideo electronic games have been confused with the real thing. A quick look at some of the other types of electronic games should clear things up for you. And it will remind you that there are an awful lot of other good games that can be cheaper and more convenient than the standard video game.

Chief source of the video/nonvideo confusion are the table-top models of popular arcade games like Bally/Midway's Pac-Man™, Galaxian™, Nintendo's Donkey Kong™, Stern's Berserk™ and Sega's Frogger™. All of these games are manufactured by Coleco.

Now here's where the confusion comes in. These are not home video versions of the games, though home video cartridges for most of these games are, or soon will be, available. Cartridges for some of the games like Donkey Kong are being offered by Coleco, which simply adds to the confusion. You can't use the Coleco table-top games with your Atari or Intellivision or even with your Coleco home video system. The games are self-contained, battery-operated versions of the arcade games. You don't attach them to your TV set. The table-top games come with their own TV screens and stand about nine inches high. The cost for these games is between $60 and $70. That's a lot more than the home video cartridges of the games, which cost $40 at most. But for someone who doesn't already have a home video system and wants to play Pac-Man or Donkey Kong, these table-top games may be a good bet. You don't have to fool around with all those wires and plugs, or hog the family TV set.

The table-top games have something else going for them—they are pretty darn good games. No, they certainly don't match the arcade games in quality or complexity. For example, the Pac-Man maze is much smaller. It has a modest 63 dots instead of the 240 in the coin-op version. The old gobbler doesn't move

COLECO
© 1982 COLECO INDUSTRIES, INC.

2390
MIDWAY'S PAC-MAN
© 1981 Coleco Industries, Inc.
Licensed by MIDWAY MFG. CO.
© MIDWAY 1981

as fast, and the cherries and other prizes simply don't exist. But the graphics are still good—surprisingly good—to many who had at first considered these table-top games mere "toys." The controls are responsive, and the sound effects first rate. The game also has variations not offered in the arcades or home video. In Eat and Run, for example, there are no dots. The gobbler must grab a power capsule and return to his home base in order to score any points.

2391 DONKEY KONG™
Electronic Arcade Game

Some even consider the table-top Pac-Man superior to Atari's home video version. It's certainly a lot of fun for younger players who want to get into Pacmania, or who want to get a taste of some of the other extremely popular arcade games without actually going to the arcade.

The table-top versions of arcade games are relatively new. Most were first introduced in 1982. Small or hand-held electronic games have been around since 1977. Until about 1980 the small games were the big sales items at Christmastime. Remember all those TV ads for the Coleco and Mattel sports games? But by 1981 these games had been completely over-shadowed by the suddenly exploding home video market. Still, a visit to any toy store will show you that the old-style electronic games are still being manufactured, and some of the old ones are fun to play. The big advantage of the hand-held models is that they are portable. You can't take your home video with you on a trip. And you can't play it while waiting in the dentist's office. So if you happen to run across an old hand-held version of Space Invaders in the back of your closet, don't throw it away.

As video games have progressed since the days of Space Invaders, so have the hand-held games. For one thing they can be made smaller. Mattel, a leader in the hand-held game field, has come out with a whole new line of what they call pocket-sized electronic games. In truth the games make a pretty big bulge in the average pocket. You wouldn't want to slip one into your back pocket and sit on it. But they are smaller than ever before, and they come with batteries included, a big plus.

The games, which have names like Armor Battle, Formula Racer and Long Bomb Foot-ball, are fairly simple and easy to play. In Formula Racer, for example, there are four buttons. One makes the car go right, another makes it go left. There is a button for breaking and a button for accelerating. The game has a small LCD display, rather like the display on a digital watch or a pocket calculator. These games resemble the pocket calculator more than anything else, although pocket calculators don't make sounds like the crashing of autos.

While the games present no great challenge to the veteran arcader, they are still a pleasant and inexpensive way to pass the time. And their portability makes them extra useful.

Mattel is offering some larger electronic games as well. World Championship Football and World Championship Baseball give you the option of playing alone or against someone else. In this same line are games that allow you to play chess or backgammon against the computer.

Mattel has been licensed by TSR Hobbies, the originators of the fantasy role-playing game Dungeons and Dragons, to produce several electronic versions of Dungeons and Dragons. One is an electronic board game in which warriorlike figures are moved across a touch-sensitive electronic board in search of a treasure guarded by a dragon. In a pocket-sized version of Dungeons and Dragons, the player tries to locate a magic arrow with which to slay the dragon—all on the LCD display.

Mattel's World Championship™ Baseball

Both of these games are entertaining in their own right, but D & D enthusiasts should not expect D & D, or even an approximation of that inventive role-playing game. D & D can not be translated into simple electronics. And some D & D freaks are outraged at the idea that electronics have been introduced into this game of the imagination. In truth, Odyssey's video game Quest for the Rings comes closer to true electronic D & D, and various computer fantasy-adventure games come closer still. Mattel has also announced that it will be marketing a home video version of Dungeons and Dragons, but as of this writing the cartridge has not been seen.

Milton Bradley, the big toy manufacturer, entered the electronic fantasy game market

Dungeons and Dragons™
computer labyrinth game from Mattel

with an attractive-looking offering called Dark
Tower. Players move pieces around a circular
board. The player has to also punch in each
move on a keyboard located on the Dark
Tower, the unit which holds the computer and

the batteries. The Dark Tower then tells the player what has happened—if he has been attacked by a dragon, or contracted the plague. Players can buy things they need, like food and warriors, by bargaining with the computer—and they can choose to fight or run. One very important thing the computer in Dark Towers does is to keep track of the progress of the game. Players are supposed to keep track of their own progress by means of a little pegboard supplied by the manufacturer. But in practice that is rarely done, and the computer has to be consulted frequently. The record-keeping duties of the computer in electronic game-playing are sometimes underrated. It's a bore to keep score, and it leads to arguments. The computer is better at the job. And you can't argue with it.

Milton Bradley is also coming out with an electronic version of its classic game Stratego, and Parker Brothers will be offering an electronic accessory for its even more classic board game Monopoly.

Every year, usually around Christmastime, the toy companies hit the stores with a hundred or so new or improved versions of electronic games. A few of the new games go on to become classics. They will be played and enjoyed for months by those who receive them. They will be sold again the following year, and for years to come. The majority of these games, however, disappear from the shelves never to be heard from again.

Almost all of the new games are fun to play—at first. But the simple electronic games are very limited. In short, they get boring fast. The games have a single purpose. With a home video game you can change cartridges when you get tired of a game. You can exchange or swap cartridges with a friend. If you don't like an electronic game it will wind up in the attic or in back of the closet. The games cost anywhere from $30 to $80. That's expensive for something you may use only a few times.

So when thinking about buying an electronic game there are several things you must keep in mind.

1. All video games are electronic. But not all electronic games are video games.
2. There are many nonvideo versions of popular video games, but don't be confused.
3. The sophisticated video-game player may find him- or herself quickly bored with most electronic games because the action is limited.
4. The games are most useful for younger players, and the portable games can be a boon when traveling or waiting somewhere.
5. If there is a game that you think you

might like, check it out carefully before you buy. Once you buy it, it's too late to change your mind. Generally the games are impossible to return unless they are broken.

6. Remember that for some popular board games, the electronic additions are just a gimmick. The games are as good, or better, in the much cheaper nonelectronic version.

7. Most of the electronic games are battery operated, and for those that use a lot of power the batteries become expensive.

8. And finally, after all that negative stuff, I would encourage the serious game player to investigate the year's crop of new electronic games anyway. The technology of these games is improving all the time. And in the mass of soon-to-be-forgotten games may be a classic or two that would be well worth having and that would make a nice break from the video games.

Speaking of gimmicks, as we were just a moment ago, modern technology has provided us with games so tiny that they can, and have, been fitted into the face of a wristwatch. People have always been doing silly things with clocks, putting cuckoos inside them or putting in dials in the form of Mickey Mouse. The game watches are just the latest in a long line of timepiece silliness—and charm.

There are so many different game watches around right now that a very brief introduction to the subject is all that we have space for. General Consumer Electronics has a very popular watch called Game Time, which contains not one but four different electronic games—Firing Squad, Missile Strike, Alien Assault and Blast Away. As you can probably guess from the titles of the games, they all involve shooting or bombing something. GCE's Arcade Time watch also features zap games, while Sports Time gives the wearer tiny versions of football, basketball and soccer along with the time and date.

No matter how miniaturized electronics become there are definite physical limits on what kind of games can be included in a wristwatch. You can't wear a watch bigger than your wrist. This has led to a revival of the old-fashioned pocket watch, the watch which, as the name implies, is carried about in the pocket. It went out with grandpa's Model T. But since pocket watches can be considerably larger than wristwatches, they have more room for games. There are now pocket watches on which you can play blackjack or poker, and even a watch where you can score points by rescuing victims of an earthquake.

Combination timepieces, pocket calculators and games are now being offered by Casio, a major manufacturer of pocket calculators, and several smaller firms.

In one way or another games seem to be getting into practically everything.

# CHAPTER 9

# THE BRAINS
# BEHIND THE GAMES

Video games don't just happen. People have to think them up. What kind of people? Some are artists and have a flair for design. Others were electrical engineers or studied computer science. Occasionally they're genius whiz kids. A few are independents, which means they're trying to work on their own. The majority work for a corporation. By and large they're on the young side, because computer technology is a new field. And since California is the place to be if you work in computers, many live there.

If you want to grow up to be a video game designer, there is no clear path for getting there. At the moment the field is overwhelmingly male, but if you're a girl, don't let that discourage you. Things are changing. A woman, Donna Taylor, programmed Atari's arcade game Centipede. As more girls play the games, companies have to create games girls like and more girls become interested in the subject.

Although going to college helps, there are video game designers who never got past high school. Some people are good at thinking up ideas but have to ask others to do the programming. Some programmers are masters at figuring out how an idea can work technologically once it's presented to them, but they couldn't create a concept on their own no matter how hard they tried.

Creating a good game really isn't easy. The best graphics in the world will not save a game if it's boring. If all you want to do is to look at a picture, you'll watch television. A video game is precisely that—a game. It must have challenge, conflict, a goal. Many arcade games have died because they're too slow or merely pretty. On the other hand, the most wonderful game will not appeal to the majority of people if it's too hard to play. And video game designers, like most people, have to worry about the practical side of what they do. Video games make money, but not all video games. No designer wants to be associated with a dud.

Then there's the level of technology the designer must work with. Although it changes quickly, nobody can afford to replace an entire home video-game system often. A designer may have a fantastic idea, but can it be programmed into, say, the Atari VCS you have at the present time in your home? There are limits on what a designer can do.

There are changes in fashion, too. Some designers can create a complex arcade video combat game with macho appeal but could never come up with a game that attracts a wide audience of different kinds of people. So there is more than simple talent involved in maintaining a spot among the top designers.

Another problem designers face is one of recognition. Except for Activision, the major companies that produce home video cartridges will not tell you who designs their games. According to *How To Master Home Video Games* by Tom Hirschfeld, Warren Robinett, who designed Atari's home video game Adventure, was so eager for some kind of recognition that he programmed a "room" into the game where you can see his name. You have to go through a series of complex maneuvers that have nothing to do with winning the game, and suddenly you see "CREATED BY WARREN ROBINETT" flash on the screen.

Why do the corporations hide their designers' names? Well, in the first place, companies want you to identify the game with them, not with the man or woman who thought the thing up. When you say Asteroids you think of Atari. There's another reason, too. Good designers and programmers are in demand, and companies are a little worried about their striking out on their own and becoming superstars. Designers might wind up like baseball players who've become free agents, worshipped by millions of kids and making big demands. They might be scooped up by rival companies.

Whether this would really happen is hard to say. Though many want higher royalties, top designers are well paid and manufacturing video games is risky. Everyone takes a gamble. It takes more than ideas to produce successful games. You need staff, equipment and a promotional campaign, the kind of things big companies are set up to do.

Still, I imagine there'll be a change. The designers of video games will begin to get some recognition. They definitely deserve it, and Activision has given it to them. So let's take a look at a few Activision designers.

Alan Miller designed Tennis, Ice Hockey and Checkers. Check the instructions on these games and you'll find he even gives you tips on playing them, but that's true in general for Activision.

Like a lot of designers he's from the West Coast. He was born in Tacoma, Washington,

Activision senior designers (from left to right)
Larry Kaplan, Alan Miller, David Crane, Steve
Cartwright and Bob Whitehead

and grew up in Newark, California. He went to
the University of California at Berkeley and
has a Bachelor of Science degree in electrical
engineering. He loves sports, so it's not sur-
prising that he designs sports games. This is
something for you to think about if, like a lot of
kids, you love sports but you're crazy about
computer science, too. You might be able to
grow up to combine both your interests.

On the personal side, when Alan Miller isn't
playing video games he likes to go to the movies. When he has to get away from it all he

heads for the out islands of Hawaii. Maybe they inspire him to think up new games.

David Crane has designed a lot of Activision games such as Fishing Derby, Dragster, Laser Blast, Freeway and Grand Prix and Pitfall! He was born in Nappanee, Indiana in 1954 but moved to California. Having an older brother who liked electronics got him involved in electronics, too. He has a Bachelor of Science degree in electrical engineering from De Vry Institute for Technology in Phoenix, Arizona. Apparently, anything stirs his fertile imagination, even an old joke about why the chicken crosses the road. The old joke wound up transformed into the home video game Freeway. He's a senior designer at Activision.

Bob Whitehead designed Skiing, Boxing, Chopper Command and one of my absolute favorite games, Stampede. Born in San Jose, California, he is married, has three kids and is very active in his church. He graduated from San Jose University in computer mathematics. Like David Crane he is a senior designer at Activision and believes that home video games make it possible for any of us, not just the technologically talented, to like computers.

Steve Cartwright is the designer of Barnstorming and Megamania, a new and extremely clever game. He, too, graduated from De Vry Institute for Technology in Phoenix,

Arizona. He's taught computer programming and electronics, was an all-star athlete in high school and loves motorcycles and photography. All you photography fans, take note.

Who knows? Maybe, someday I'll be writing about you and the game you designed. It really could happen.

# CHAPTER 10

# FUTURE GAMES

In 1972 there was Pong. Now look at the video game field. No one could have predicted the way it would grow and change over the past ten years. There is no reason to believe that change stops here and now. Major new developments are on the drawing board. Some of them we have already discussed. In this chapter we are going to look a little further into the future and try and explore some of the trends in video games. We will try to see what the games will be like ten years or more from now.

Practically everyone agrees that the biggest and most obvious changes are going to be in graphics. Already a game like Kick Man looks a lot like an animated cartoon.

Of course, the cartoon style will not necessarily triumph over all else. Take a game like Atari's Yars' Revenge. Its graphics are beautiful but highly abstract. Whether cartoon or abstract, the graphics of the games both at home and in the arcades will be more striking and vivid than ever before.

A glimpse of the arcades of the future can already be seen in the Magic Kingdom's Tomorrowland Starcade. There will be more giant screen games, or cockpit style games—games that you can actually sit in and be surrounded by screens that create the feeling of being right in the middle of the action.

Today pilots are trained on a simulator. It is a cockpit device in which all of the sights and sounds of actual flying can be duplicated. The pilot trainee can suddenly be faced with an emergency like a crash landing without actually being in danger. The feel of these training simulators is astonishingly realistic. Many in the video game field believe that future games will be able to duplicate the kind of effects found today in the flight simulator. Not only will the player be surrounded by visual images and sounds, but the cockpit itself will shake or turn over or do whatever is required.

For example, if you are playing a space battle game and your ship is hit, the flash will surround you and you will be able to actually feel the vibrations.

In the large arcades the games of the future may not be self-contained. They may be controlled by a central computer. This will enable them to produce effects much more complex than those available today.

It's a glorious future. But there's a fly in the ointment—the cost. Some of the newer and more elaborate games already cost fifty cents in many arcades. It's not hard to foresee games that will be gulping dollars, not quarters.

The real future of the video games may be at home. Companies like Atari are already coming out with improvements on their basic system. All sorts of accessories—better joysticks, keyboards and the like are coming onto the market. But the development of the home video game as strictly a game unit has its limits. The game unit itself can become so complex and expensive that you have to ask yourself, Why not buy a computer? Why not, indeed?

In the future computers may be as common in the home as television sets are today. If that's the case, most home games will be played on them. That opens up a whole new range of games that can be played. And you won't have to plug all those wires into your TV set. That is, unless you have one of those wall-sized screens that are now becoming popular.

Rich Tarbell

How would you like to play Pac-Man on one of those! One day you probably will.

TV will enter the video game field in another way. There are already a few cable TV stations that allow two-way communication between the station and the viewer. Some of these stations have been offering video games to subscribers on an experimental basis. The graphics for the game are broadcast from the TV studio. With the proper equipment they can be picked up and played at home.

One advantage of this system is that new games can come out very, very quickly. Just a few weeks after the war between Britain and Argentina over the Falkland Islands broke out, there was a cable TV station offering a game based on the war. It wasn't much of a game. And it was quickly withdrawn. People didn't like the idea of making a game out of a real war. But that will give you some idea of how fast a new game can be brought to the public through cable TV. The video game of the future may be very timely. Perhaps people will be able to try out games on TV first. It will be like records. First you hear a number on the radio. If you like it enough you go out and buy the record.

How about the movies? The movies are frankly worried about the video games explosion. Movies were badly hurt by the development of TV. You can't go to a movie while watching TV. And you can't go to a movie while you are in the arcade or playing games at home, either.

The movies have tried their best. Some movie theaters have installed coin-op games in the lobby. Sometimes people seem more interested in what's going on on the screen in the lobby than what's going on on the screen in the theater.

Movie tie-ins are the next step. Walt Disney Production's *Tron* is the first major movie with a video game theme. In the movie both the hero and the villain are transported into the world of the computer, and they fight it out in a video game landscape. Many of the most striking effects in the film were designed by computer. The Bally coin-op game and the two Mattel Tron cartridges are based on the film. Filmgoers will instantly recognize the world of Tron in the game. And game players will see their own fantasies of being totally immersed in an electronic game come to life on the movie screen.

By Christmas 1982 another major video game movie, *Starblasters,* should be out. If these movies are successful you can expect a flood of video game movies and games based on the movies. In fact, there are already a number of games out or planned that are based on, or named after, popular films. One of the

Solar Sailor from the film *Tron*

first was Atari's Superman. There is also Parker Brothers' The Empire Strikes Back. There are plans for games based on *Raiders of the Lost Ark* and *Conan*.

The enormous success of video games may change the whole concept of entertainment. Aside from the games, much of our entertainment is passive. We sit and look at a movie or a TV show. We read a book. We may find the movie, show or book absorbing or entertaining. We react to it. But we can't affect it. We can affect the outcome of a video game. We are not just observers, we are participants.

In a letter to the *New York Times Magazine*, James R. Beninger, an assistant professor of sociology at Princeton University, suggests that perhaps video games have given us "a taste for something new"—movies or TV shows that we can affect. We don't just sit and watch, we actually participate, just as we do in a video game.

There are already several series of children's books in which readers can direct the plot and choose the ending. They are very much like the text adventure games played on computers.

Professor Beninger points out that there are two-way cable TV systems which have experimented with giving viewers a choice of endings to TV dramas. He suggests that with computer technology viewers can be offered "hundreds of variations on plots."

Someday you may be able to play a game in which Dracula or Darth Vader really is your opponent.

# CHAPTER 11

# HOW TO FIND OUT MORE

As I have said at least a dozen times, the video game industry is new. It's changing all the time. There are a number of publications that regularly print news and information about the games. Most of these publications are what is known as trade magazines. They are written for people who are in the video game business.

There is, however, one good general publication, *Electronic Games*. It covers not only arcade and home video games but also computer games and nonvideo electronic games as well. The magazine reviews new games, tells you what to expect next and gives advice to players in a bright and breezy style.

For example, a reader named Mo from Ontario wrote to a regular column conducted by "the Game Doctor" that he was running his Intellivision for ten to twelve hours a day and "its brains get hot." Mo wanted to know if he should move the power supply outside to cool off.

The answer was: "Ten to twelve hours!?! Holy hi-res, Mo, you really ought to give that poor master component a rest cure. Maybe send it to Saskatoon—or someplace else cool—for prolonged vacation. Ten or twelve hours!?????!!

"Even today's more durable computers are extremely sensitive to heat, and running them for marathon play sessions such as yours would melt anyone's brains. Remember, moderation is the key to enjoyment and happiness. There is a danger in too much of a good thing. Consider it a little Rx from the Game Doc. You'll get my bill next week."

Oh, yes, the bill—that's the one drawback for this dandy little magazine. It costs $2.95 an issue on the newsstands. It has just gone monthly and the subscription price is $28 a year.

The address is:

Electronic Games
235 Park Avenue South
New York, NY 10013

*Electronic Games* does not hesitate to criticize new games or equipment when necessary. But you must remember that the magazine is supported by electronic game industry advertising. That simply has to influence the magazine's outlook. So before you make a major investment, let us say in a new home video computer system, you might be wise to check and see if a noncommercial publication like *Consumer Reports* has rated the equipment. *Consumer Reports* usually rates various sorts of games in its November issue just before Christmas every year. You can also check the annual buying guide published by the magazine.

The address is:

Consumer Reports
256 Washington Street
Mt. Vernon, NY 10550

There are a lot of books around that will tell you how to master or beat the various games. Quite frankly, I do not like that approach. In most cases it is quite misleading. It's like a book on how to master juggling. The books can give you some basic pointers, but you will never learn to juggle by reading a book. What you must do is practice, practice, practice.

Many games have slight flaws in the program—cheats, they are called. If you know the cheats in a particular game you may be able to get ahead without really playing the game. That seems unfair and takes a lot of the fun out of playing. It's a bit like reading the last page of a mystery story before you have made a guess as to whodunit. If you discover the cheats on your own, great—it can give you a real sense of accomplishment. But it takes no skill in playing the game to read about them in a book. Besides, tips like that are not as helpful to most players as you may think. You already have to be very skillful to make use of the tricks. With most home video cartridges the manufacturers supply a sheet of instructions and tips that will allow you to play the game adequately. In the arcades you really have to watch the good players before attempting a new game.

Still, books on how to beat or master various games are extremely popular. Here are a couple that are easily available, and might be useful. Tom Hirschfeld has written two books: *How to Master the Video Games* and *How to Master the Home Video Games*. Both are published by Bantam and cost $2.95. Both cover the games popular in 1981. A more recent book is *How to Win Video Games,* by the Editors of Consumer Guide (Pocket Books, $2.95).

**117**

Craig Kubey's *The Winners' Book of Video Games* (Warner Books, $5.95) contains tips on popular arcade and home video games as well as some background information and jokes. *Video Invaders,* by Steve Bloom (Arco, $5.95 in paperback) also contains a mixture of tips and video game information.

Some people like to contact manufacturers directly for information on home video games or equipment. The addresses for the big three among the manufacturers are:

Atari, Inc.
1265 Borregas Avenue
Sunnyvale, CA 94086

Mattel, Inc. (Intellivision)
5150 Rosencrans Avenue
Hawthorne, CA 90250

Magnavox (Odyssey)
P. O. Box 6950
Knoxville, TN 37914

There are a growing number of software manufacturers, but the largest at present is Activision. It is also the friendliest. Activision prides itself on establishing a personal relationship with its customers by sponsoring clubs, publishing a newsletter for game fans, publicizing the names of its designers and generally

trying to shed the image of corporate imper-
sonality.
  Their address is:

>     Activision
>     2350 Bayshore Frontage Road
>     Mountain View, CA 94043

## ABOUT THE AUTHOR

DANIEL COHEN's books are popular with young readers and reviewers alike. A former managing editor of *Science Digest,* Mr. Cohen has written extensively on science topics, supernatural occurrences and the occult. His interest in video games was sparked by their unique combination of technology and fun. Mr. Cohen is a frequent lecturer at college campuses throughout the United States and Canada, and has often discussed his ideas and interests on radio and television.

Mr. Cohen's first book, *Myths of the Space Age,* was published in 1967, and since then he has written more than seventy-five books for adults and children—several of which have won awards.

Daniel Cohen was born in Chicago and has a degree in Journalism from the University of Illinois. He and his wife Susan, also a writer, their daughter Theodora, and several dogs and cats live in Port Jervis, N.Y.